She Who Sees
The World

Isle of Eigg

Christine Morro

She Who Sees the World — Isle of Eigg
©2023, Christine Morro

Books may be purchased in quantity and/or special sales by contacting the publisher. All inquiries related to such matters should be addressed to:

Middle Creek Publishing & Audio
9161 Pueblo Mountain Park Road
Beulah, CO 81023
editor@middlecreekpublishing.com
(719) 369-9050

First Paperback Edition, 2024
ISBN: 978-1-957483-05-4

All Photography: Christine Morro

She Who Sees
The World

Isle of Eigg

Christine Morro

Middle Creek Publishing & Audio
Beulah, CO USA

"Crossing water always furthered something"

Seamus Heaney

From the east June 2022

MONE | MOON

Full moon

Dark fissile

mudstone

inside the raven winged house

bog and cushions of cow dung

forager of purslane   feet raw cold as wet earth

ebbing tide   far off poems on the breath

three million years to grow

Recognizing sands

dreamed by our ancestors

The living body of earth

sings hymns of rock weed

Forests of kelp

Between worlds

Sea ensky'd

Encoded wisdom

How do we learn to listen

SWIFF: a hollow mellow sound made by wind

BASALT SILLS

Soft shales yield fossils

Grassy talus

Who asks us to listen

A stone dropping through water

SHE WHO SEES THE WORLD

I have forgotten

so long

wiped clear

Rocks become words

Seaweed syntax

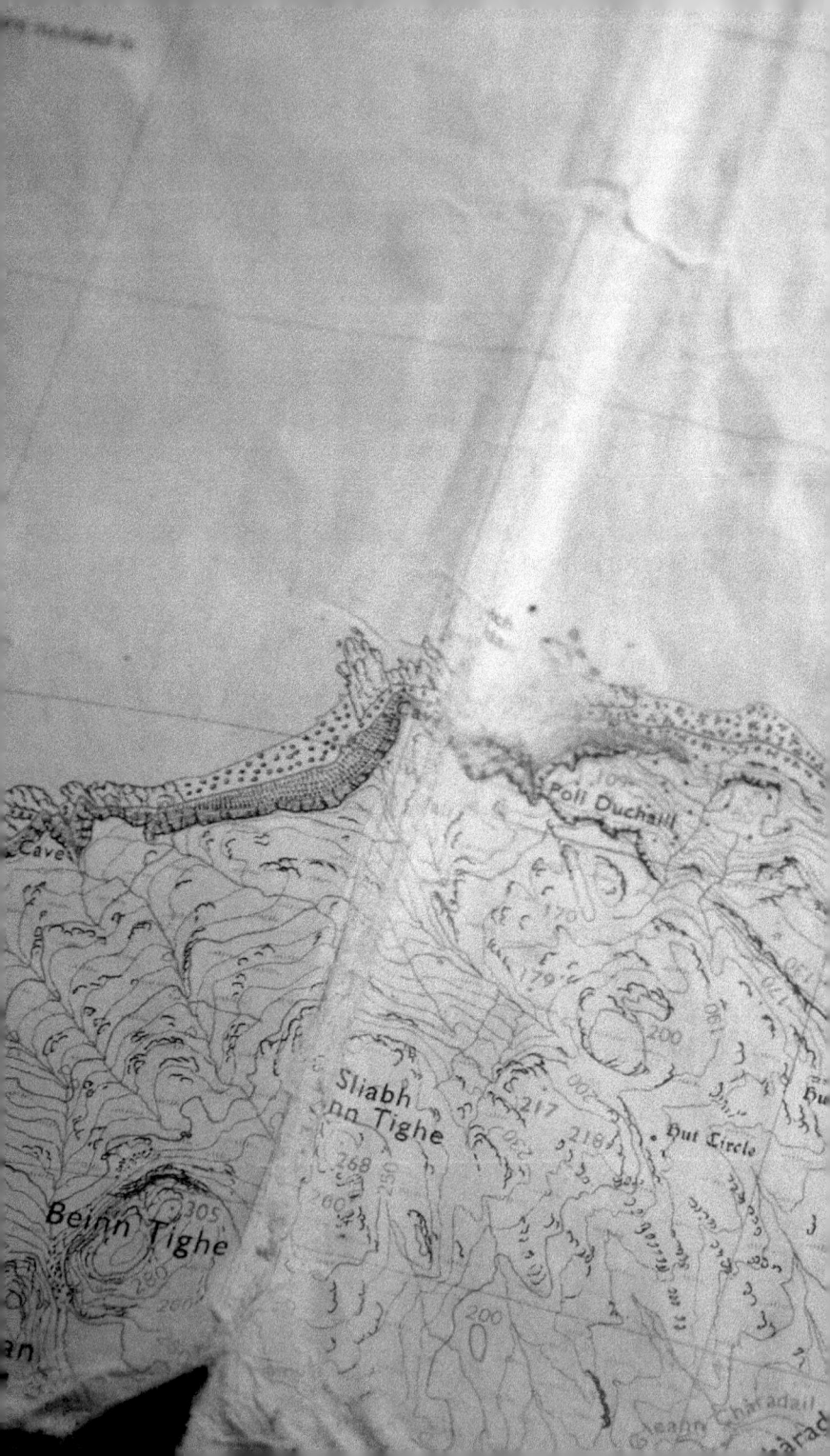

Cave

Poll Duchaill

170

179

200

217

218

Sliabh
nn Tighe

305
280

Hut Circle

268
200

Beinn Tighe
280
200

200

Gleann Charadail

Bay of Laig

Sgòrr Tuathach

Sgòrr Chaoruil

Sgòrr Mòr
Sgòrr na Tràghar

Cnoc
Mòr
Meall
Cave
Druim
Chòirce

Tràigh Chlithe

Corrairigh

Laig

Sidhean na
Cailleich

Druim an Lochain

Abhainn a' Ghlaic Còs

Sgòr
Làimhrige

Quarry
(dis)

Allt a'
Bhealaich Chlithe

Waterfalls

Hut Circles

Cleieh Mhòr

Waterfall

Bealach Airigh
an Leir

FBs

Cam Lòn

Blàr Dubh

WALKS FROM SWEENEY'S BOTHY

TO CAMAS SGIOTAIG, SINGING SANDS,

ISLE OF EIGG

A

VIEW OF

ISLE OF RUM

FROM LAIG BAY

C

A I

R N

S

T O N

E S

bludie bells | fox glove

king cups | marsh marigold

aaron's beard | st. john's wort

buckie brier | wild rose

buckie faalie | primrose

buck beard | moss

hare bell | blue bell

Told in green, fern

And rain

Mist cloaked

SMIRR: a trace of rain in the wind

Hours move like water

memory of flow

inside cliffs of basalt

ragged clouds

days unsealed

approaching solstice

Stone guardian

protector of all who arrive

with cupped hands and kneel

before the holy well

Courting solitude

oh, beautiful and strange

escorted by watery spirits

into the land's dreaming

Among moss and lichen

heel of twilight

Silent on the edge

of shadows

Short-eared owl

SCOVE:

To fly equally, smoothly

To poise on the wing

stripped bare

bone cave

transmitted through

fragments of shells, quartz

dark shale and limestone

tell me from the beginning

Unveil the vast tidal space,

Between this world and the next

Chant these songs

back to earth

Oh ebbing sea

To break open, down

through genealogy

to geology

from timelines

to memory maps of song

A recess in stone

rainwater font

deeper form of touching earth

wings, scales, algal and fluid

return to kindom

e ar t h s e a ai r

A littoral correspondence

Eros of Place

Weight of stone on my palm

memory of earth   the bones

of my pelvis remember

Great cave of belonging

Tidal rhythms attended

by an assembly of

M

O

O

N

S

HORIZON

The weight of grey born of the edge of the world

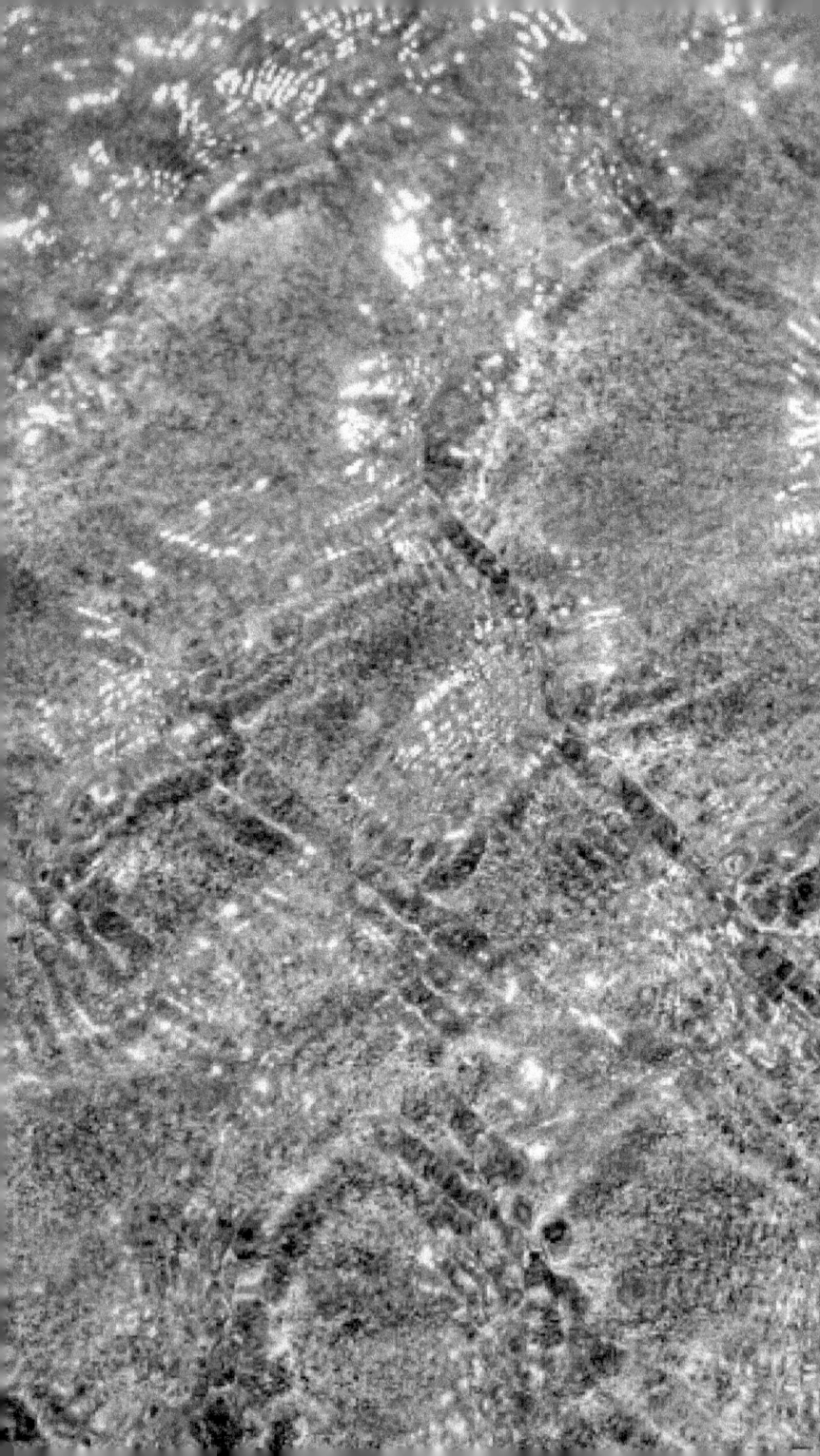

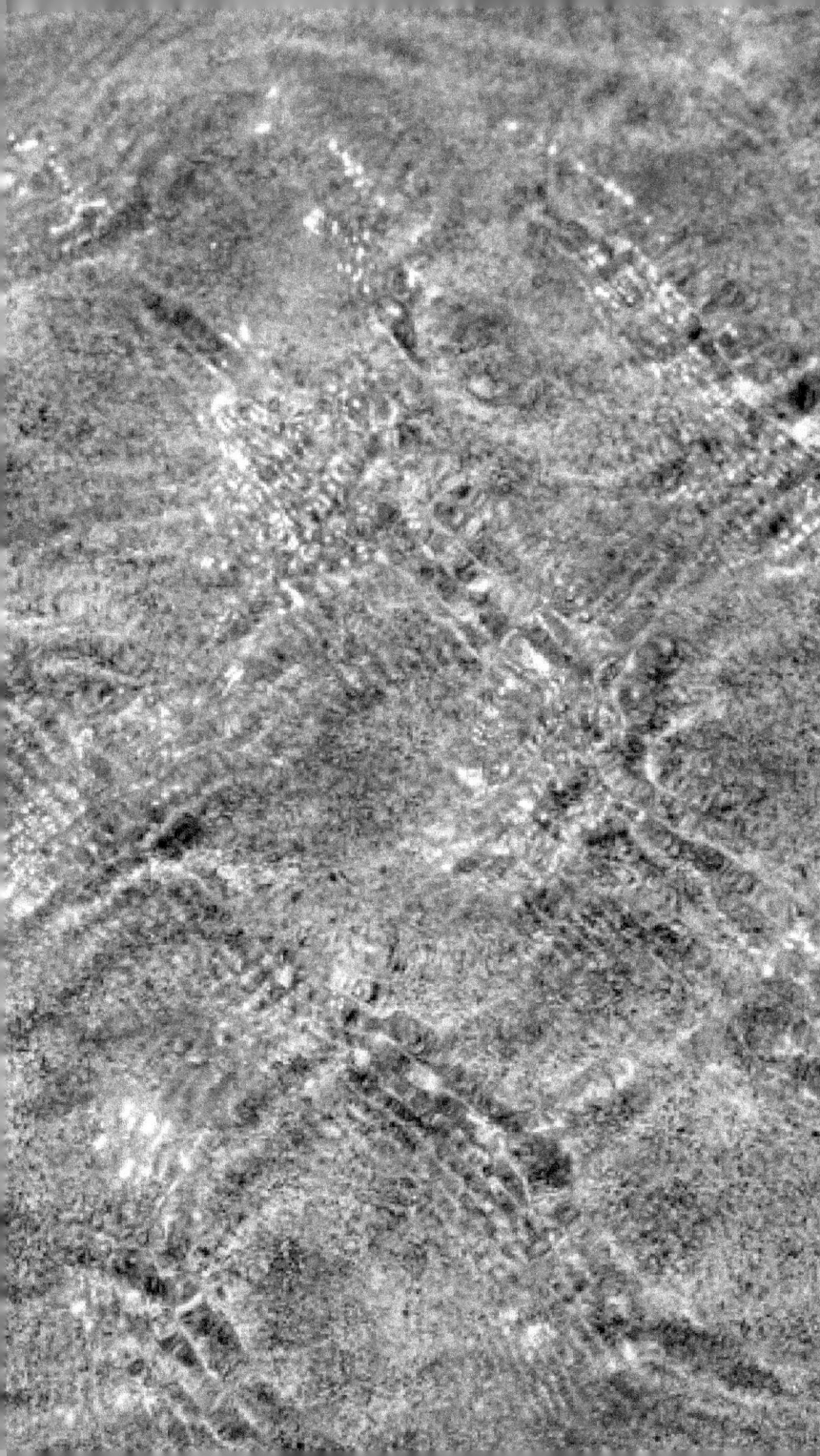

remembered into being

a kaironic reweaving

Suibhne *we are myths unfolding*

For all who cross the threshold

into the imaginal

The many doors encountered

eyes, ears, skin, nose, mouth

The winds, the tides of the sea

The moon

Ferry journeys no matter how long their duration represent a crossing into the imaginal, the elusive and unknown.

Approaching Isle of Eigg, the pre-solstice sun, wings of light the distance though only 16 miles from the mainland becomes arbitrary, what is quantifiable slips away.

I understand I will be changed by this land.

In the distance the isle appears like an ancient cetacean, a mythic creature rising out of the Hebridean Sea. My eyes follow the contour of its back as it narrows to its tail. I know very little of the land known as *Eilean Eige*, old Norse for notch, wedge. As we move closer toward port, the landscape suddenly gleams with a vibrance of green that feels otherworldly. My whole being wants to sing. *An Sgurr*, a dramatic stump of pitchstone stands, a grandfatherly guardian.

Day by day I walk. Dark shales, sandstone, limestone, siltstone, basalt express themselves in the continuum of deep time. The earth is changing and though the geologic bodies of Eigg speak of endurance I sense an urgency to listen. I stand still. It begins with my breath before I hear the slow external pulse.

Earth insistent we again receive the elemental codes. Her wisdom transmitted moment by moment available not by outsourcing our authority but by placing palms to ancient ground. Accepting the invitation to be a part of the currency of life.

The earth, the great waters know only generosity.

June 2022

Sweeney's Bothy
Isle of Eigg, Scotland

Christine Morro

About the Author

Walker, listener, intuitive | each morning a beginner.

Christine Morro writes poetry and creates art informed by the anima of the natural world, inspired by the sacred in the ordinary, the flight of shorebirds and the just after. Enlarged by encounters with the more than human world she seeks to enter this opening through a weaving back into our ecomythological story — to live the question how to belong to earth. Her writing is an offering to readers in the form of prayers, poems, incantations. A reminder to keep pace with the rhythms and cycles of earth, to navigate with attention.

Christine's poetry has appeared in *Reliquiae* (Corbel Stone Press); her prose and photography have appeared in *Minding Nature,* (Center for Humans and Nature), Landlines (Leeds University UK), *The Pilgrim, Flyway Journal* and *River Heron Review*. Her debut collection, *In Beauty We Are Made Visible* was published in 2022 by Middle Creek Publishing & Audio.

christinemorro@gmail.com
www.christinemorro.weebly.com

About The Press

Middle Creek Publishing believes that responding to the world through art & literature — and sharing that response — is a vital part of being an artist.

Middle Creek Publishing is a company seeking to make the world a better place through both the means and ends of publishing. We are publishers of quality literature in any genre from authors and artists, both seasoned and those who are undiscovered or undervalued, or underrepresented, with a great interest in works which illuminate or embody any aspect of contemplative Human Ecology, defined as the relationship between humans and their natural, social, and built environments.

Middle Creek Publishing's particular interest in Human Ecology is meant to clarify an aspect of the quality in the works we will consider for publication and as a guide to those considering submitting work to us. Our interest is in publishing works which illuminate the Human experience through words, story or other content that connects us to each other, our environment, our history, and our potential deeply and more consciously.

www.ingramcontent.com/pod-product-compliance
Lightning Source LLC
Chambersburg PA
CBHW071358090426
42738CB00012B/3152